50 Delicious Rice Bowl Recipes for Summer

By: Kelly Johnson

Table of Contents

- Grilled Chicken Teriyaki Rice Bowl
- Shrimp and Avocado Rice Bowl
- Mango Coconut Rice Bowl
- Teriyaki Salmon Rice Bowl with Veggies
- Thai Red Curry Vegetable Rice Bowl
- Chipotle Chicken Burrito Bowl
- Beef Bulgogi Rice Bowl
- Mediterranean Quinoa and Brown Rice Bowl
- Zucchini and Corn Summer Rice Bowl
- Sriracha Tofu Rice Bowl with Broccoli
- Lemon Garlic Herb Chicken Rice Bowl
- Crispy Chickpea Buddha Bowl
- Pineapple Fried Rice Bowl
- Caprese Rice Bowl with Fresh Basil
- Sweet and Sour Chicken Rice Bowl
- Sesame Ginger Chicken Rice Bowl
- Korean BBQ Pork Rice Bowl
- Smoked Salmon Rice Bowl with Cream Cheese
- Lentil and Brown Rice Bowl with Spices
- Spicy Tuna Poke Rice Bowl
- Mediterranean Chicken Rice Bowl with Hummus
- Buffalo Cauliflower Rice Bowl
- Sushi Rice Bowl with Fresh Vegetables
- BBQ Chicken Rice Bowl with Corn Salsa
- Caribbean Jerk Chicken Rice Bowl
- Eggplant and Chickpea Rice Bowl
- Fish Taco Rice Bowl with Cabbage Slaw
- Cilantro Lime Rice Bowl with Black Beans
- Curry Chicken and Rice Bowl
- Quinoa, Brown Rice, and Black Bean Bowl

- Roasted Vegetable and Feta Rice Bowl
- Peach and Chicken Rice Bowl
- Sesame Noodle and Rice Bowl
- Stuffed Bell Pepper Rice Bowl
- Teriyaki Portobello Rice Bowl
- Greek Rice Bowl with Feta and Olives
- Savory Egg Fried Rice Bowl
- Crispy Garlic Shrimp Rice Bowl
- Harvest Bowl with Roasted Squash and Kale
- Chili Lime Fish Rice Bowl
- Saffron Chicken Rice Bowl
- Spring Vegetable Rice Bowl
- BBQ Pulled Pork Rice Bowl
- Chickpea and Spinach Rice Bowl
- Coconut Curry Lentil Rice Bowl
- Tomato Basil Rice Bowl with Mozzarella
- Pork and Pineapple Rice Bowl
- Stuffed Avocado Rice Bowl
- Cilantro Lime Shrimp Rice Bowl
- Grilled Vegetable Rice Bowl with Balsamic Glaze

Grilled Chicken Teriyaki Rice Bowl

Ingredients

- 2 chicken breasts
- 1/2 cup teriyaki sauce
- 2 cups cooked jasmine rice
- 1 cup broccoli florets
- 1 bell pepper, sliced
- 1 carrot, julienned
- 2 green onions, sliced
- Sesame seeds for garnish

Instructions

1. **Marinate Chicken**: In a bowl, combine chicken breasts with teriyaki sauce. Let marinate for at least 30 minutes.
2. **Grill Chicken**: Preheat the grill to medium-high heat. Grill chicken for 6-7 minutes on each side, or until cooked through. Let rest for a few minutes before slicing.
3. **Sauté Vegetables**: In a skillet, add a splash of water and steam broccoli, bell pepper, and carrot until tender, about 5-7 minutes.
4. **Assemble Bowls**: In serving bowls, place a scoop of jasmine rice. Top with sliced grilled chicken and sautéed vegetables.
5. **Garnish**: Sprinkle with green onions and sesame seeds. Drizzle with additional teriyaki sauce if desired.

Enjoy your delicious Grilled Chicken Teriyaki Rice Bowl! Let me know if you need any more recipes or adjustments!

Shrimp and Avocado Rice Bowl

Ingredients

- 1 lb shrimp, peeled and deveined
- 2 cups cooked brown rice
- 1 avocado, sliced
- 1 cup cherry tomatoes, halved
- 1 lime, juiced
- Salt and pepper to taste

Instructions

1. In a skillet, cook shrimp over medium heat until pink, about 3-4 minutes.
2. In a bowl, combine cooked brown rice, shrimp, avocado, and cherry tomatoes.
3. Drizzle with lime juice and season with salt and pepper. Toss gently and serve.

Mango Coconut Rice Bowl

Ingredients

- 2 cups cooked jasmine rice
- 1 cup coconut milk
- 1 ripe mango, diced
- 1/4 cup shredded coconut
- 1 tablespoon honey (optional)

Instructions

1. In a saucepan, heat coconut milk and honey until warm.
2. Mix warm coconut milk into cooked jasmine rice.
3. Serve topped with diced mango and shredded coconut.

Teriyaki Salmon Rice Bowl with Veggies

Ingredients

- 2 salmon fillets
- 1/2 cup teriyaki sauce
- 2 cups cooked jasmine rice
- 1 cup steamed broccoli
- 1 cup sliced carrots

Instructions

1. Marinate salmon fillets in teriyaki sauce for 30 minutes.
2. Preheat the grill or oven and cook salmon until flaky, about 6-8 minutes.
3. Serve over jasmine rice with steamed broccoli and carrots.

Thai Red Curry Vegetable Rice Bowl

Ingredients

- 1 cup cooked jasmine rice
- 1 can (14 oz) coconut milk
- 2 tablespoons red curry paste
- 2 cups mixed vegetables (bell peppers, snap peas, carrots)
- Fresh basil for garnish

Instructions

1. In a pan, heat coconut milk and red curry paste until combined.
2. Add mixed vegetables and cook until tender.
3. Serve over jasmine rice and garnish with fresh basil.

Chipotle Chicken Burrito Bowl

Ingredients

- 2 chicken breasts, cooked and shredded
- 2 cups cooked brown rice
- 1 cup black beans, drained
- 1 cup corn
- 1 avocado, diced
- Salsa and lime wedges for serving

Instructions

1. In a bowl, layer brown rice, shredded chicken, black beans, corn, and diced avocado.
2. Top with salsa and serve with lime wedges.

Beef Bulgogi Rice Bowl

Ingredients

- 1 lb beef, thinly sliced
- 1/2 cup soy sauce
- 1 tablespoon brown sugar
- 2 cups cooked rice
- 1 cup sliced cucumbers
- Sesame seeds for garnish

Instructions

1. In a bowl, mix soy sauce and brown sugar, then marinate beef for 30 minutes.
2. Cook marinated beef in a skillet over medium-high heat until cooked through.
3. Serve over rice, topped with cucumbers and sesame seeds.

Mediterranean Quinoa and Brown Rice Bowl

Ingredients

- 1 cup cooked quinoa
- 1 cup cooked brown rice
- 1/2 cup chickpeas, rinsed and drained
- 1/2 cucumber, diced
- 1/2 cup cherry tomatoes, halved
- 1/4 cup feta cheese, crumbled
- Olive oil and lemon juice for dressing

Instructions

1. In a large bowl, combine cooked quinoa, brown rice, chickpeas, cucumber, cherry tomatoes, and feta cheese.
2. Drizzle with olive oil and lemon juice, then toss to combine.

Let me know if you need any more recipes or adjustments!

Zucchini and Corn Summer Rice Bowl

Ingredients

- 1 cup cooked rice
- 1 zucchini, diced
- 1 cup corn (fresh or frozen)
- 1 bell pepper, diced
- 1 tablespoon olive oil
- Salt and pepper to taste

Instructions

1. In a skillet, heat olive oil over medium heat. Add zucchini, corn, and bell pepper. Sauté until tender, about 5-7 minutes.
2. Combine sautéed vegetables with cooked rice. Season with salt and pepper. Serve warm.

Sriracha Tofu Rice Bowl with Broccoli

Ingredients

- 1 block firm tofu, pressed and cubed
- 2 cups cooked rice
- 1 cup broccoli florets
- 3 tablespoons Sriracha sauce
- 1 tablespoon soy sauce

Instructions

1. In a skillet, cook cubed tofu until golden brown on all sides.
2. Add broccoli and cook until tender. Stir in Sriracha and soy sauce, mixing well.
3. Serve tofu and broccoli over cooked rice.

Lemon Garlic Herb Chicken Rice Bowl

Ingredients

- 2 chicken breasts, cooked and sliced
- 2 cups cooked rice
- 1 lemon, juiced
- 2 cloves garlic, minced
- 1 tablespoon fresh herbs (parsley or basil), chopped

Instructions

1. In a bowl, combine sliced chicken with lemon juice, garlic, and fresh herbs.
2. Serve over cooked rice, drizzling with any remaining lemon juice.

Crispy Chickpea Buddha Bowl

Ingredients

- 1 can chickpeas, drained and rinsed
- 2 cups cooked quinoa or brown rice
- 1 cup mixed greens
- 1 avocado, sliced
- Olive oil, cumin, and paprika for seasoning

Instructions

1. Preheat the oven to 400°F (200°C). Toss chickpeas with olive oil, cumin, and paprika, then bake for 20-25 minutes until crispy.
2. Assemble bowls with quinoa or rice, mixed greens, sliced avocado, and crispy chickpeas on top.

Pineapple Fried Rice Bowl

Ingredients

- 2 cups cooked rice
- 1 cup pineapple chunks (fresh or canned)
- 1/2 cup peas and carrots
- 2 tablespoons soy sauce
- 2 green onions, sliced

Instructions

1. In a skillet, sauté peas, carrots, and pineapple until heated through.
2. Add cooked rice and soy sauce, mixing well. Cook for an additional 3-4 minutes.
3. Serve topped with sliced green onions.

Caprese Rice Bowl with Fresh Basil

Ingredients

- 2 cups cooked rice
- 1 cup cherry tomatoes, halved
- 1 cup fresh mozzarella balls
- Fresh basil leaves
- Balsamic glaze for drizzling

Instructions

1. In a bowl, combine cooked rice, cherry tomatoes, mozzarella balls, and fresh basil.
2. Drizzle with balsamic glaze and serve.

Sweet and Sour Chicken Rice Bowl

Ingredients

- 2 chicken breasts, cubed
- 1 cup bell peppers, chopped
- 1 cup pineapple chunks
- 1/2 cup sweet and sour sauce
- 2 cups cooked rice

Instructions

1. In a skillet, cook cubed chicken until browned. Add bell peppers and pineapple, cooking until tender.
2. Stir in sweet and sour sauce and heat through. Serve over cooked rice.

Let me know if you need any more recipes or adjustments!

Sesame Ginger Chicken Rice Bowl

Ingredients

- 2 chicken breasts, sliced
- 2 cups cooked rice
- 1/4 cup soy sauce
- 2 tablespoons sesame oil
- 1 tablespoon fresh ginger, grated
- 1 cup broccoli florets
- Sesame seeds for garnish

Instructions

1. In a skillet, heat sesame oil over medium heat. Add sliced chicken and cook until browned.
2. Add soy sauce, grated ginger, and broccoli. Cook until broccoli is tender.
3. Serve over cooked rice and garnish with sesame seeds.

Korean BBQ Pork Rice Bowl

Ingredients

- 1 lb pork tenderloin, sliced
- 1/2 cup Korean BBQ sauce
- 2 cups cooked rice
- 1 cup shredded carrots
- 1 cup sliced cucumbers

Instructions

1. Marinate sliced pork in Korean BBQ sauce for at least 30 minutes.
2. Cook marinated pork in a skillet until cooked through.
3. Serve over cooked rice, topped with shredded carrots and sliced cucumbers.

Smoked Salmon Rice Bowl with Cream Cheese

Ingredients

- 2 cups cooked rice
- 4 oz smoked salmon
- 1/4 cup cream cheese, softened
- 1/2 cucumber, thinly sliced
- Fresh dill for garnish

Instructions

1. In a bowl, spread cream cheese over the cooked rice.
2. Top with smoked salmon, cucumber slices, and fresh dill. Serve chilled.

Lentil and Brown Rice Bowl with Spices

Ingredients

- 1 cup cooked lentils
- 1 cup cooked brown rice
- 1 teaspoon cumin
- 1 teaspoon paprika
- Salt and pepper to taste
- Fresh parsley for garnish

Instructions

1. In a bowl, mix cooked lentils and brown rice.
2. Add cumin, paprika, salt, and pepper. Mix well.
3. Serve garnished with fresh parsley.

Spicy Tuna Poke Rice Bowl

Ingredients

- 1 lb sushi-grade tuna, cubed
- 2 cups cooked rice
- 1 avocado, sliced
- 1/4 cup soy sauce
- 1 tablespoon sriracha
- Green onions for garnish

Instructions

1. In a bowl, combine cubed tuna, soy sauce, and sriracha.
2. Serve over cooked rice, topped with avocado slices and green onions.

Mediterranean Chicken Rice Bowl with Hummus

Ingredients

- 2 chicken breasts, cooked and sliced
- 2 cups cooked rice
- 1/2 cup hummus
- 1/2 cup cherry tomatoes, halved
- 1/2 cucumber, diced
- Olive oil and lemon juice for drizzling

Instructions

1. In a bowl, layer cooked rice, sliced chicken, hummus, cherry tomatoes, and cucumber.
2. Drizzle with olive oil and lemon juice before serving.

Buffalo Cauliflower Rice Bowl

Ingredients

- 1 head cauliflower, chopped
- 1/2 cup buffalo sauce
- 2 cups cooked rice
- 1/4 cup blue cheese dressing
- Green onions for garnish

Instructions

1. Preheat the oven to 425°F (220°C). Toss cauliflower in buffalo sauce and spread on a baking sheet. Roast for 25-30 minutes.
2. Serve roasted cauliflower over cooked rice, drizzled with blue cheese dressing and garnished with green onions.

Let me know if you need any more recipes or adjustments!

Sushi Rice Bowl with Fresh Vegetables

Ingredients

- 2 cups sushi rice, cooked
- 1 avocado, sliced
- 1 cucumber, julienned
- 1 carrot, shredded
- 1/4 cup soy sauce
- 1 tablespoon sesame seeds

Instructions

1. In a bowl, layer cooked sushi rice, avocado, cucumber, and shredded carrot.
2. Drizzle with soy sauce and sprinkle sesame seeds on top before serving.

BBQ Chicken Rice Bowl with Corn Salsa

Ingredients

- 2 chicken breasts, grilled and sliced
- 2 cups cooked rice
- 1 cup corn (fresh or canned)
- 1/2 cup diced tomatoes
- 1/4 cup chopped cilantro
- 1/4 cup BBQ sauce

Instructions

1. In a bowl, mix corn, diced tomatoes, and cilantro to create the salsa.
2. Serve sliced chicken over rice, topped with corn salsa and BBQ sauce.

Caribbean Jerk Chicken Rice Bowl

Ingredients

- 2 chicken breasts, marinated in jerk seasoning
- 2 cups cooked rice
- 1/2 cup black beans
- 1/2 cup diced mango
- Lime wedges for serving

Instructions

1. Grill or bake the marinated chicken until cooked through.
2. Serve sliced chicken over rice, topped with black beans and diced mango. Garnish with lime wedges.

Eggplant and Chickpea Rice Bowl

Ingredients

- 1 eggplant, diced
- 1 can chickpeas, drained and rinsed
- 2 cups cooked rice
- 1 teaspoon cumin
- 1 teaspoon paprika

Instructions

1. In a skillet, sauté diced eggplant until soft. Add chickpeas, cumin, and paprika, cooking until heated through.
2. Serve over cooked rice.

Fish Taco Rice Bowl with Cabbage Slaw

Ingredients

- 1 lb white fish (like tilapia), cooked and flaked
- 2 cups cooked rice
- 1 cup shredded cabbage
- 1/4 cup lime juice
- 1/4 cup chopped cilantro

Instructions

1. In a bowl, mix shredded cabbage with lime juice and cilantro to create the slaw.
2. Serve flaked fish over rice, topped with cabbage slaw.

Cilantro Lime Rice Bowl with Black Beans

Ingredients

- 2 cups cooked rice
- 1 can black beans, drained and rinsed
- 1/4 cup cilantro, chopped
- Juice of 1 lime

Instructions

1. In a bowl, combine cooked rice, black beans, cilantro, and lime juice. Mix well.
2. Serve warm.

Curry Chicken and Rice Bowl

Ingredients

- 2 chicken breasts, cooked and cubed
- 2 cups cooked rice
- 1 cup coconut milk
- 2 tablespoons curry powder
- 1 cup mixed vegetables (peas, carrots, etc.)

Instructions

1. In a skillet, combine coconut milk and curry powder, bringing to a simmer. Add mixed vegetables and cooked chicken.
2. Serve over cooked rice.

Let me know if you need any more recipes or adjustments!

Quinoa, Brown Rice, and Black Bean Bowl

Ingredients

- 1 cup quinoa, cooked
- 1 cup brown rice, cooked
- 1 can black beans, drained and rinsed
- 1/2 cup corn (fresh or canned)
- 1/4 cup cilantro, chopped

Instructions

1. In a bowl, combine cooked quinoa, brown rice, black beans, and corn.
2. Toss with chopped cilantro before serving.

Roasted Vegetable and Feta Rice Bowl

Ingredients

- 2 cups mixed vegetables (bell peppers, zucchini, carrots), roasted
- 2 cups cooked rice
- 1/2 cup crumbled feta cheese
- Olive oil for drizzling

Instructions

1. In a bowl, layer cooked rice and roasted vegetables.
2. Top with crumbled feta and drizzle with olive oil before serving.

Peach and Chicken Rice Bowl

Ingredients

- 2 grilled chicken breasts, sliced
- 2 cups cooked rice
- 1 ripe peach, sliced
- 1/4 cup balsamic glaze

Instructions

1. In a bowl, layer cooked rice, sliced chicken, and peach slices.
2. Drizzle with balsamic glaze before serving.

Sesame Noodle and Rice Bowl

Ingredients

- 2 cups cooked noodles (like soba or rice noodles)
- 2 cups cooked rice
- 1/4 cup soy sauce
- 1 tablespoon sesame oil
- 1 cup shredded carrots
- Sesame seeds for garnish

Instructions

1. In a bowl, mix cooked noodles and rice. Add soy sauce and sesame oil, tossing to combine.
2. Top with shredded carrots and sprinkle sesame seeds before serving.

Stuffed Bell Pepper Rice Bowl

Ingredients

- 4 bell peppers, halved and seeded
- 2 cups cooked rice
- 1 cup cooked ground beef or turkey
- 1 cup marinara sauce
- 1/2 cup shredded cheese (mozzarella or cheddar)

Instructions

1. In a bowl, mix cooked rice, ground meat, and marinara sauce.
2. Fill each bell pepper half with the mixture, top with shredded cheese, and bake at 375°F (190°C) for 20 minutes until peppers are tender.

Teriyaki Portobello Rice Bowl

Ingredients

- 4 portobello mushrooms, grilled
- 2 cups cooked rice
- 1/4 cup teriyaki sauce
- 1 cup steamed broccoli

Instructions

1. In a bowl, layer cooked rice, grilled portobello mushrooms, and steamed broccoli.
2. Drizzle with teriyaki sauce before serving.

Greek Rice Bowl with Feta and Olives

Ingredients

- 2 cups cooked rice
- 1/2 cup kalamata olives, pitted and sliced
- 1/2 cup cherry tomatoes, halved
- 1/2 cup crumbled feta cheese
- 1/4 cup olive oil and lemon juice dressing

Instructions

1. In a bowl, combine cooked rice, olives, cherry tomatoes, and crumbled feta.
2. Drizzle with olive oil and lemon juice dressing before serving.

Let me know if you need any more recipes or adjustments!

Savory Egg Fried Rice Bowl

Ingredients

- 2 cups cooked rice (preferably cold)
- 2 eggs, beaten
- 1 cup mixed vegetables (peas, carrots, corn)
- 2 tablespoons soy sauce
- 1 tablespoon sesame oil

Instructions

1. In a large skillet, heat sesame oil and scramble the beaten eggs until cooked.
2. Add cooked rice and mixed vegetables to the skillet, stirring well.
3. Drizzle with soy sauce and cook until heated through, then serve.

Crispy Garlic Shrimp Rice Bowl

Ingredients

- 1 lb shrimp, peeled and deveined
- 2 cups cooked rice
- 4 cloves garlic, minced
- 2 tablespoons olive oil
- 1/4 cup green onions, chopped

Instructions

1. In a skillet, heat olive oil and sauté minced garlic until fragrant.
2. Add shrimp and cook until pink and crispy.
3. Serve shrimp over rice, garnished with chopped green onions.

Harvest Bowl with Roasted Squash and Kale

Ingredients

- 2 cups roasted butternut squash, cubed
- 2 cups cooked rice
- 2 cups kale, sautéed
- 1/4 cup walnuts, chopped
- Balsamic vinaigrette for drizzling

Instructions

1. In a bowl, layer cooked rice, roasted squash, and sautéed kale.
2. Top with chopped walnuts and drizzle with balsamic vinaigrette before serving.

Chili Lime Fish Rice Bowl

Ingredients

- 1 lb white fish (like tilapia), cooked and flaked
- 2 cups cooked rice
- 1 avocado, sliced
- 1/4 cup chopped cilantro
- Juice of 1 lime
- 1 tablespoon chili powder

Instructions

1. In a bowl, layer cooked rice, flaked fish, and avocado slices.
2. Sprinkle with chili powder, cilantro, and lime juice before serving.

Saffron Chicken Rice Bowl

Ingredients

- 2 chicken breasts, cooked and sliced
- 2 cups cooked rice
- 1/2 teaspoon saffron threads, soaked in 2 tablespoons warm water
- 1/4 cup peas
- 1/4 cup almonds, slivered

Instructions

1. In a bowl, mix cooked rice with saffron water and peas.
2. Top with sliced chicken and slivered almonds before serving.

Spring Vegetable Rice Bowl

Ingredients

- 2 cups cooked rice
- 1 cup asparagus, chopped
- 1 cup snap peas
- 1/2 cup green onions, sliced
- 1 tablespoon olive oil

Instructions

1. In a skillet, heat olive oil and sauté asparagus and snap peas until tender.
2. Serve sautéed vegetables over cooked rice, topped with sliced green onions.

BBQ Pulled Pork Rice Bowl

Ingredients

- 2 cups cooked rice
- 1 lb pulled pork, cooked
- 1/2 cup BBQ sauce
- 1/4 cup coleslaw

Instructions

1. In a bowl, layer cooked rice and pulled pork.
2. Drizzle with BBQ sauce and top with coleslaw before serving.

Let me know if you need any more recipes or adjustments!

Chickpea and Spinach Rice Bowl

Ingredients

- 2 cups cooked rice
- 1 can chickpeas, drained and rinsed
- 2 cups fresh spinach
- 1/4 cup tahini or your favorite dressing
- Lemon wedges for serving

Instructions

1. In a bowl, combine cooked rice, chickpeas, and fresh spinach.
2. Drizzle with tahini or dressing, and serve with lemon wedges.

Coconut Curry Lentil Rice Bowl

Ingredients

- 2 cups cooked rice
- 1 cup cooked lentils
- 1 can coconut milk
- 2 tablespoons curry powder
- 1 cup chopped spinach

Instructions

1. In a saucepan, combine coconut milk and curry powder, and heat.
2. Stir in cooked lentils and spinach until heated through.
3. Serve over cooked rice.

Tomato Basil Rice Bowl with Mozzarella

Ingredients

- 2 cups cooked rice
- 1 cup cherry tomatoes, halved
- 1/4 cup fresh basil, chopped
- 1/2 cup mozzarella balls
- Olive oil for drizzling

Instructions

1. In a bowl, mix cooked rice with cherry tomatoes, basil, and mozzarella.
2. Drizzle with olive oil before serving.

Pork and Pineapple Rice Bowl

Ingredients

- 2 cups cooked rice
- 1 lb pork tenderloin, cooked and sliced
- 1 cup fresh pineapple, diced
- 1/4 cup teriyaki sauce

Instructions

1. In a bowl, layer cooked rice, sliced pork, and diced pineapple.
2. Drizzle with teriyaki sauce before serving.

Stuffed Avocado Rice Bowl

Ingredients

- 2 ripe avocados, halved and pitted
- 2 cups cooked rice
- 1 can black beans, drained and rinsed
- 1/2 cup corn
- Salsa for topping

Instructions

1. In a bowl, mix cooked rice, black beans, and corn.
2. Stuff avocado halves with the mixture and top with salsa before serving.

Cilantro Lime Shrimp Rice Bowl

Ingredients

- 1 lb shrimp, peeled and deveined
- 2 cups cooked rice
- 1/4 cup cilantro, chopped
- Juice of 1 lime
- 1 tablespoon olive oil

Instructions

1. In a skillet, heat olive oil and cook shrimp until pink.
2. Serve shrimp over cooked rice, garnished with chopped cilantro and lime juice.

Grilled Vegetable Rice Bowl with Balsamic Glaze

Ingredients

- 2 cups cooked rice
- 2 cups assorted grilled vegetables (zucchini, bell peppers, eggplant)
- Balsamic glaze for drizzling

Instructions

1. In a bowl, layer cooked rice and grilled vegetables.
2. Drizzle with balsamic glaze before serving.

Let me know if you need more recipes or adjustments!

www.ingramcontent.com/pod-product-compliance
Lightning Source LLC
LaVergne TN
LVHW081335060526
838201LV00055B/2670